Buy a car in an hour or less

John Earl

ISBN-10: **1492204455**

ISBN-13: **978-1492204459**

John Earl

Introduction

Case study, Anita:

A Single mom of two just got bad news from the mechanic.

Anita takes her car to the dealer where she bought it because she thinks they give better service than the independent mechanics out there, even though she knows they charge a little bit more.

Her 1997 Chevy Astro van needs a water pump, timing belt and brakes, and that's just to keep it on the road for another couple months when she'll need to spend another $1,500.00 to fix the transmission. What should she do?.....should she spend 1800 bucks now and then throw another 1500 at it again in a month? Well, she decides, maybe I'll just get a new car.

Into the showroom she walks and meets Barry the new car salesman at New Age motors, here to help her get into a new car. Six hours later she heads home exhausted and $4,000.00 poorer, with monthly payments of $600 for her new minivan.

What happened you ask? Anita got "pounded" as they say in the car business. The salesman made a $700 commission, and the dealership made a $4,500 front end gross profit on her, not counting the $1,200 they made on the new car warranty, the $400 they made on the paint sealant and alarm plus the $1,800.00 they made in finance reserve. The dealership made over $8,000.00 profit on poor Anita and she'll be paying for it for the next 72 months (that's 6 years folks!)

When she goes to trade in this car that she paid about $50,000.00 for over the 6 years she drives it, it will be worth 3,500.00 bucks maybe,......sound like a great idea?...no, me neither.

Buying a new car sucks, I know it does. You're going to be dealing with some guy who could care less about your financial situation or your bills. All he cares about is stuffing you into a something he has "in stock" and sending you home in a car today.

I'm writing this book to help you navigate the nightmare of walking into a car dealership, and to show you how to buy a car within an hour or less and walk away knowing you didn't get taken advantage of.

Deciding on what kind of car to get is probably the most important decision you can make when starting the car buying process because it will set the foundation for all your car purchases going forward, think of it like a long chain and at every link you get to drive an exciting new automobile. Your life is going to change over the next 10, 20, 30 years and this will not be the last car you buy. If you make smart decisions about cars now you'll be able to upgrade, down grade and fill every need you and your family may have over your lifetime and maybe eventually end up with that fancy Hummer you've been longing after (I'm kidding, don't ever buy a Hummer) but before we do that you need to know how these guys operate and what their mentality is so that you know who you're dealing with and how not to get caught up in their drama.

I was born into the car business. My father was a car dealer; my grandfather was a car dealer. I started washing cars at my dad's store when I was 12 years old during summer vacations, I've worked in every department in a car dealership and I can tell you how they all work. As a car salesman I've sold as many as 75 cars in a month and averaged over 30 a month for a long time. As a New Car Sales Manager I witnessed and participated in some very unbecoming behavior while working car deals. I became uncomfortable with the mentality of "Car Guys" driven by ego and barracuda-like competition. The business model is archaic and hopefully something better is emerging driven by informed and pro-active consumers.

Even with the advent of the Internet and the amount of information available about actual dealer costs on cars most salesmen or managers don't care about customer service or customer loyalty. This may not be the case in all dealerships but is certainly far too rare. They want to make as much money as they can on you today and don't care if you come back the next time you need a car. Their self worth is directly tied to how many cars they move and how much money they can make on a car deal. They will brag about how hard they pounded a customer for days after a big sale. Clearly, your welfare takes a back seat to their standing in a small circle of salesmen.

That's not to say that a dealership is not allowed to make a profit, they are. I just think that if they're willing to take a 1,000 dollar profit on a car that they shouldn't make a 10,000 profit on some poor guy just because they can. There's nothing admirable in gouging people, especially those it might affect the most like poor Anita!

The End came for me after I'd been working in the same dealership for over 10 years. I was doing well as a fleet manager with over 90% of my business being repeat or referral and I really didn't care how much I made on each sale. Sometimes I made a lot and sometimes only a 100 bucks per car, didn't really matter when I was selling 40 a month. I made a good living, but the thing that got to me was the attitudes of the upper management. I became the consumer advocate and had to fight for my customers. The battles were daily and ruthless; I was called "weak" and a "give away artist "yet I was selling 3 and 4 times as many as the next guy.

The dealership had done nothing to help me cultivate my client base; I had done it with honesty and integrity and was seeing the fruits of my labor in the form of corporate and business accounts as well as individuals who bought multiple cars each year. But the management wasn't satisfied. They thought that with as many cars as I sold I should be putting more gross (profit) on the books. They didn't understand that the foundation of good business is "win win", not "hammer every person that walks through the door". The business I brought into the store was free!, it didn't cost a penny to make my phone ring, it was all word of mouth, while they we're spending $50,000.00+ a month to get someone to walk into the showroom via advertising in print and on radio.

I finally had had enough of the daily fighting over why my customers didn't want to pay an extra thousand dollars for car alarms and paint sealant and I quit. While I figure out what the next chapter of my life holds I figured I would help you not get "pounded" the next time you buy a car. I'd be happy to help you personally but hopefully after reading this little book you'll have the confidence to try it yourself with success!

The Set Up

A car dealership is like a castle. The King is the sales manager and he sits in the glass tower in the center of the showroom overlooking the kingdom (the showroom). He is the one responsible for making the car deals and has all the power to say yes or no to a transaction. The salespeople are the sentries and they guard the Castle and protect the king. You (the customer) are not allowed to talk to the king, only the salespeople are allowed to talk to the king and they better not piss him off. If they come to the king without a commitment to buy a car today or with a stupid question they are in big trouble and he may split their car deal with another salesperson, cutting their commission in half! The salespeople fear the king.

The sentries or salespeople stand guard in front of the showroom and make sure no one gets in or out without permission. You've seen it, the group of guys standing in front of the showroom waiting for their turn to talk to someone. That someone is you and you're called an "Up", salesmen are serious about "Ups". I call it "The Gauntlet" They're like a band of evil marauders in bad suits waiting for a passing caravan to pillage. Salespeople will get in big trouble if someone leaves without permission, or if they are looking at cars by themselves for more than 2 minutes without anyone talking to them.

The sentry's job is to make you fall in love with a new car and get you into the showroom to a little desk where they can get a commitment out of you to buy a car today. The salesperson presents your offer to the king; he says no and sends the salesperson back with a counter offer much higher than your original offer. This will take place a few times while you sit trying vainly to kill time, then when you all finally agree on terms of a sale the king sends all your personal information to a business manager who will type up a contract and your motor vehicle registration information, then try to sell you additional worthless products like paint and fabric protection and a car alarm that you can buy from the guy down the street for a quarter of what the dealer is trying to sell it to you for.

By now you're worn out, you've been there for 3 hours and you just want to get this over with and go home.

Tomorrow morning you'll wake up with a sick feeling in your stomach and look at the new car sitting in your driveway wondering if you paid too much or if you got taken advantage of. You did both of those things.

Car Salesmen, or Liners we call them, are under tremendous pressure from their managers to sell cars now; not tomorrow or next week but today, now, while you're here. They work on the front line, hence the name, and they are who you first meet when you go to a car dealership. They have no authority to make any decisions or commit to any price whatsoever. They have several jobs that range from moving cars around the lot to going and buying the sales mangers lunch or picking up dry cleaning, but their most important job is to "call ups"

The Archaic System

It's a system that has been honed for years and it starts the minute you pull up in your car. I've seen cars pull in, take a look at the gauntlet, turn around and leave, that's how imposing it is. I've stood in the gauntlet too. It's amazing to me that the owner of the store lets this take place but they do. Other stores have a system in place where they at least let you get out of the car and walk toward the showroom before someone approaches you. What they've done is move the gauntlet inside the showroom and a computer tells the salesmen whose turn it is. They wait patiently for a customer to pull in and park, then pounce on them.

The dealer may have a system in place for the "Ups" but it may be a free-for-all as well, I've seen fist fights break out over "Ups". "You stole my up!" is usually how it starts. When one salesman steals another salesman's customer it's called "Skating", "You skated me on that deal" is another cry heard often in a car dealership and another fist fight may likely take place somewhere on the back lot.

Another big misnomer about the car business is the word "DEAL". "I'll get you a good deal" they say, or your friend tells you what a great deal he got from so and so. Don't believe it!

Basic Economics

The car business is like any other business in that they are there to make a profit. They buy something for a certain price and then sell it for more than they paid for it, very simple. Keep this in mind as you read. What happens is people get caught up in the hype—in the word "deal." A car deal is literally what we call the actual folder we put your paperwork in to move it around the dealership, from the sales manager to the finance guy to the business office and then to a storage facility in the attic.

There are no deals! The only real deals are from the manufacturer or the bank. For instance when the manufacturer puts a zero percent interest rate on a car, that came from the bank not the dealer. The same is true for cash incentives; you've heard it on the radio "get $1,000.00 cash back on a new truck". That was put up by the manufacturer not the dealer. The dealer is still going to make money on the car and the incentive the auto maker put in place has nothing to do with the price the dealer is willing to sell you the car for. Make sense?

Deal Structure

The deal encompasses the whole transaction, the structure. Dealers use a complicated computer program to determine leasing and loan payments. The programs are excellent and make it easy for sales managers to determine car payments. They simply plug in all the info.

Sale price of the car, interest rate, trade value (and payoff if there is one). The program adds sales tax and license fees and tells them what the payment is. It also tells them exactly how much money they're making on any given transaction or "deal". This is called a deal structure and the structure is what you care about, how much are we getting on our trade in? What's the finance rate and if we're leasing what's the money factor and residual?

I just had a conversation with an old customer who called me because her lease was up and she needed a new car. I suggested I negotiate for her, she told me the dealer had been calling her and that there's a "deal" going on. I told her not to believe them, but she did anyway and never told me she was going in to get a new car. I called my buddy over there at the dealership after not hearing from her for a couple days and sure enough, they got her. I could have saved her several hundred dollars more than what she paid and the dealer would have still been happy to do the deal. Of course I didn't tell her this because I didn't want to upset her. She didn't get hosed exactly because she's smart, but I still could have saved her more money.

So what happens after you pull up and walk to the showroom? Once you're "Upped" by the salesman he's with you until you "buy or die" as they say, and if you give him your phone number his boss will make him call you every day until you tell him you've bought a car or your relatives tell him you have died. The dealer may even have a sophisticated system in place (a boiler room) that your information will be entered into for continued daily harassment until you "Buy or Die".

If you fall into this trap you're screwed. They will try to keep you in the dealership for as long as they can and even steal the keys to your car or your driver's license in order to prolong your agony. And, if you don't buy a car on this visit they'll low ball you as walk out the door. "Don't pay more than $250 a month for that new Honda" they'll say. It happens all the time. The low ball plants the seed and when no other dealer comes close to that number hopefully they can lure you back so they can take one last crack at you.

The goal when buying a car is not necessarily to get the best possible price, you can always get a better price, and I'll talk more about this later too. The goal is to get a good price on a car and not waste hours doing it. I can certainly think of better places to spend my free time than a car dealership.

So, what's the first thing you need to do when it's time to get a new car? Read on.

What kind of car should I get, and what do I do first?

Case Study Jesse: *29 year old personal trainer with 2 year old daughter.*

Jesse came to see me the other day driving her two and half year old Audi A4. Black and sleek, the car was beautiful.

"Jay, you have to help get me out of this car," she pleaded. "Why Jess? Car looks great." I wondered.

'This car is a piece of shit, Jay. I've only had it for 2 1/2 years and the headlights keep burning out, the sunroof doesn't work anymore and I just got a new customer who lives 30 miles away and I need better mileage."

I had in fact told Jesse this when she mentioned getting the Audi.

The problem: Jesse still had 2 ½ years to go on her payments and the car is now not worth nearly what she owes the bank on it. This is called being "upside down". You don't ever want to be upside down in your car when it's time to trade ... ever!

There are two things you need to do and know before you even think about going to a dealership, one is decide what kind of car you want to get and two, decide how you're going to pay for it. In order to decide how you're going to pay for it you need to know what your credit looks like. Once you know what your credit score is you'll know what your options are and can act accordingly. We'll discuss credit in a minute but first, the car.

When I was selling cars I would always ask what kind of car the customer is currently driving and if they like it, first off it tells me a lot about the customer and secondly it would help me sell my brand.

Of course they all said they loved their current car. I would then ask if they'd had any problems with it. "No,' they usually said "it's been great." Of course nobody wants to admit they made a poor decision. What I found is that after a little probing they did have problems with it. I also found that a lot of people come to think of car repairs as normal because cars break down. I'm here to tell you that you can get a car that will not break down and that will not need thousands of dollars in repairs after it hits 60k miles. There's a reason why the Toyota Camry is the best selling sedan in the United States and it's not because it's so stylish, it's because it's good.

With so many choices out there now it can be tough to decide what kind of car to get. By making a smart choice on what kind of car to buy (or lease) you can increase the amount of money that goes into your pocket or retirement fund instead of the mechanics pocket.

I love cars and have my whole life. I think there is nothing prettier than red a Ferrari or the new Porsche Panamera. But is that what I would go get if I we're a single mom? No. How about that cute new VW Jetta? Nope, not unless you want to spend hours at the dealership arguing with the service guy about why the warranty on some items expires after the first year.

There are several things to consider when deciding what car to choose. That hot little Audi might be fine if you're going to keep the mileage low and don't mind leasing, but if you're buying a car to be practical and want it to last then an Audi is not for you.

Unless you're financially independent or have a sugar daddy then you're going to have to put your ego aside here. Cars are not an investment. Worth saying again. CARS ARE NOT AN INVESTMENT. Cars are a necessary evil of being independent.

They are a necessary evil of living in a city with poor public transportation too. In order to maintain a financially stable existence you need a dependable car that will not break down or be expensive to maintain. Look at it like part of your monthly budget. Make an allowance for it. Even if it's paid off you need to allow for maintenance and repairs. What are you going to do when the water pump goes out? The smart thing to do is have an emergency fund of at least a $1,000.00 and not just for the car. You should have an emergency fund anyway and having a reliable, good quality car will help you build that fund. Imagine 4 or 5 years of hassle free driving, where you didn't spend a penny on vehicle repairs. I haven't spent one dime on repairs for my car in the time I've owned it. Only oil changes and regular maintenance.

So what kind of car should you get? Well, it should probably be Japanese. Overall they are the best cars made in the world. And Honda and Toyota are the best Japanese cars made. Also, both Honda and Toyota have factories in the US so you don't really need to be worried about "buying foreign." As a matter of fact some major American brands have as much or more "foreign content" than these so called Japanese brands. Ford and VW both make cars in Mexico or Canada now. You can rest easy knowing you are supporting American jobs here at home, and that's not to say that the other manufacturers aren't making good cars. They have improved dramatically but still fall behind the top end Japanese brands. Some Korean brands are becoming more popular and might be a good buy but they are lacking in some of the safety categories and reliability is still a question with Hyundai and Kia, but worth keeping an eye on.

You'll need to go drive one of each if you're torn, and we'll talk about how to do that without getting hassled in the next chapter

Japanese. It's the way to go, I promise!

Another question is what model? Sedan, SUV, Van, Hybrid? Only you can answer these questions but some things to think about.

Do you have any kids or plan to have any? Are you going to change jobs anytime soon that might require more driving? Do you haul stuff? Are you going to be making more or less money in 3 to 5 years?

I'm not going to tell you how much car to get or what portion of your monthly budget you should allocate to a car payment, just remember that the car Is not the only thing that you have to pay for in dealing with transportation, there's insurance and yearly registration, not to mention the maintenance and upkeep.

You should have a plan in regard to your automotive needs just like you have a plan in regard to your home ownership or career path. Are you on the upward trajectory or closer to retirement? This will most likely not be the last car you buy. You're going to have to either sell it, trade it or turn it in at some point. Of course we can never predict a depression or recession like the one we just experienced but I would err on the side of caution. My income decreased by more than half after 2008 and while I've made some poor financial decisions in my life choosing and buying cars hasn't been one of them. .

Stick to the basics or "There's no accounting for taste"

There is a saying in the car business "there's an ass for every seat" and this phrase was generally used when there was an oddball car on the lot. The purple Ford Pinto with the pink interior that's been there for nine months, well, there's an ass for that seat. Don't let that ass be yours. Even if they offer you what looks like a ridiculous deal, stick to cars in primary colors (white, silver, gray, black) and standard options as these will be easier to move and garner better money on a trade in later down the road. While we are on the topic, the best indication of a good quality, reliable car is the resale value. Research how much are they selling for used.

A word about Hybrids

I love them. They seem to be reliable now that they've been around for over 10 years and you can't beat the gas mileage. I wouldn't necessarily get a bigger hybrid, meaning the vans or bigger SUVs, but the hybrid sedans are great. If you're thinking about a hybrid, you have to go with Toyota. They make the best in the world and license their technology to other manufacturers like Ford and Nissan. Be smart; go with the leader in this technology. Hybrids typically get almost double the gas mileage you would get out of a mid-sized sedan. Take a Toyota Camry for example. The EPA says it gets 25 miles a gallon in the city and 35 miles a gallon on the highway. If you're like most people you do more city driving than highway and remember the EPA estimates are always a little higher than what you actually get. Let's say you get 28 miles a gallon combined in your real world. A Toyota Prius gets about 42 miles a gallon in real world city driving and even better on the highway. With gas at 4 bucks a gallon and up nowadays you can see the savings. I would venture to guess that you'll save no less than a 100 bucks a month in gas and maybe even as much as 200-250 a month if you do a lot of driving. That's real money that you'll notice in your pocket friends. Get a hybrid if you can.

A quick note about gas mileage. The EPA is the one who puts the mileage estimates on cars, not the car maker. When Hybrids first came out I heard stories of people complaining about the actual gas mileage the cars were getting and I have to say it annoyed me a little. These are people who never checked their gas mileage before buying a car that was purported to get 50 miles a gallon and they were angry that it was only getting 40. They never checked the mileage they were getting when they were driving the SUV that was getting 14 miles a gallon, and now they're mad that Toyota and Honda Hybrids weren't getting the 50 miles a gallon that it said it would on the window sticker? Please!

A few years back the EPA changed the method they used to estimate gas mileage on new cars and they've become much more realistic, but gas mileage is still affected by your driving habits and road conditions. People only became aware of these things when hybrids hit the scene. I think that due to the increased awareness in real world gas mileage results the EPA was pressured into updating their testing methods. It's about time.

Should I get a used car?

You can absolutely get a great used car that will be just as reliable as a new car. With the introduction of the "Certified Pre-Owned" programs that most manufacturers offer and the warranties that accompany them you're in great shape to get a used car. The pricing will be lower but overall not to the extent you might think. Look at it like this: you can get the same new model you're looking at in a used car but it will have more options. For example instead of the base model Honda Accord, you can get the EX model instead but it's going to have 30-50k miles on it. If you don't drive that much and you're not going to put 20,000 miles year on it then it's something to think about. I would absolutely think about getting a used car, maybe something a couple years old with low mileage.

There are several websites that have great information about new and used vehicles.

Consumerreports.com is a subscription based site that takes no advertising dollars and hence is not biased towards any particular brand.

Edmunds.com is another good resource

KBB.com: Kelly blue book, a great resource for how vehicles are equipped in your particular region. (You need to know how they are configured in order to get accurate quotes)

What About My Credit?

Once you decide what kind of car you think you might want you need to know what your credit looks like. There is nothing more appealing to a car dealer than someone with edgy credit. They literally start salivating when they see a low credit score because they know they can probably get you financed but oooh....it's gonna cost you.

It puts them totally in the driver's seat because you now need them to help you, and believe me they have no desire to help you unless there's something in it for them. Meaning, a nice profit on the car, a nice profit on the financing and the fact that you will be required to purchase that expensive extended warranty that's going in the deal whether you like it or not.

Go to one of the online credit bureaus and run your credit.

Experian.com or one of the other credit reporting companies.

The credit score you get from these online services may not be the exact score that the dealer will pull when he runs your credit but it will at least give you an idea of what your score should be. Anything over 720 is excellent and will qualify you for the best programs that the manufacturer may be offering in incentives.

If your credit score is on the lower side I would look into finding my own financing either through a credit union or my own bank. You can even secure financing over the Internet thru several online banks. Once you know what kind of interest rate you can get from a third party it gives you a bargaining chip when you're at the dealer. Give them a chance to beat your rate and now they're working for you. It changes the dynamic of the whole transaction to your favor.

The dealer is going to run your credit but don't let them do it until you're ready to buy.

Fact: the dealer, by law, is required to tell you what your credit score is.

How are you going to pay for it?

Lease or buy? Finance or pay cash?

Case Study:

Warner: 42 years old, owns 3 restaurants and expanding!

I've known Warner now for several years and he always buys his cars, doesn't believe in leasing because you never own anything and always have a car payment.

On his way to bring his car in for service he got in an accident. He was fine but the car wasn't. The insurance company decided not to total the car but to fix it instead. I had urged Warner to get the insurance company to total it out but they wouldn't. The car ended up costing over $11,000.00 to fix. (The original estimate was $8,000.00 which is always the case.)

When Warner wanted to get a new car I had the unfortunate task of having to explain to him why his car was only worth $5,000.00 on trade instead of the $9,000.00 he thought he would get for it.

It was because it had been wrecked and repaired. Once a car has been repaired by a body shop the value decreases significantly, by half in some cases, and it takes about 30 seconds for an experienced used car manager to tell when a car has been in an accident.

Warner never bought another car, he leased every one of them

There's a few ways to go about this financing business, and leasing is just another form of financing by the way, invented by a guy as a way to sell more cars....it works.

First off I'll say that if you have the money to pay cash in full for a car then do it. There's no sense in paying interest on an item that depreciates in value. But, if the manufacturer is offering 0% interest or even 1% interest then you may as well use the bank's money and not yours. Go ahead and finance it. You might want to finance the whole purchase and not put any money down. Why not? Its free money! But I generally suggest you put at least the tax and license down, there's no reason to pay interest on tax and government fees.

Let me back up a little bit here for the people that may not know. When you buy a car there are fees associated with it. Just like any other item you buy there is sales tax. Here in California right now it's as high as 9%. Along with tax you'll be charged a registration fee for the license plate or DMV fee, this is good for only the first year at which time you'll have to renew it. And there will most likely be a doc fee, I don't really know what this fee is for but it's anywhere from $75 to $110.00 depending on where you buy the car, and you can't get out of it. They say it's for the processing of your paperwork at the DMV but it may go straight into the dealership owner's pocket for all I know. So, when you're negotiating the purchase of a car, say a cash deal, you want an "out the door price" that means you want the price with all fees and taxes included. Fortunately, the dealers can't fudge on these fees, they are what they are and you can't get out of them, but by negotiating your best price on the car you can minimize the amount of tax and license you pay. Obviously the lower the price the car is the lower the fees will be.

I know that most people are not in the position to plunk down $30k or 40k in cash at one time so financing is going to come into play and leasing might be the best option. Leasing in and of itself is not a good or a bad thing, it really depends on your individual circumstances. I hear it all the time "well you never own the car" this is true, but remember that even when you buy a car it's not really yours until you've made that last payment to the bank which might be 5 or 6 years down the line. You know what your car is worth in 5 or 6 years? That's right. Not much. From my experience most people are in the market for a new car every four and half years or so, even if they buy their cars (not lease).

Remember, the value in an automobile is in the service that it provides to you in reliability and economy. When you lease a car you generally get more bang for your buck, meaning that you can get more car than you would if you bought it.

Here's how leasing works: The bank guesses what the vehicle will be worth in a given amount of time, generally 3 years. On a good quality car It's usually somewhere around 50% of the sticker price, and they give this to you up front essentially. They call this the residual and it's the amount that you can buy the vehicle for at the end of the lease term if you want to. Hence, you're only paying for about half the car. Now the payments aren't going to be half what they would be if you bought it because there's still interest to be paid but, you can get a significantly more expensive car for the same money. Sound appealing? You bet it does and dealerships lease lots of car. There are tax advantages too. Talk to your accountant about it. You may be able to write off the whole lease payment or at least a good portion of it. Also, you only pay sales tax on the monthly payment, not the whole car. The tax is paid monthly along with your payment. Consequently lease payments are always quoted "plus tax"

After 3 years you have the option to buy the car at the residual value or turn it in and get another one

Benefits to leasing:

Your car is under warranty the whole time you drive it.

Scheduled maintenance is included in some cases.

You get to drive a new car (it's not going to break down)

If you should get in an accident, the bank assumes the liability not you.

Disadvantages of leasing:

Mileage restriction: you're only allowed to drive a certain amount of miles over the term of the lease (but you can set the mileage limit)

You'll always have a car payment

Might be tougher to qualify for a lease

So... should you lease or buy?

If you're on a really limited monthly budget I would think hard about leasing instead of buying. The payment will be lower, you'll be driving a new car that is covered under warranty for at least most if not the entire term of the lease, you won't have any unexpected repair bills to think about, which, if you own your car outright can and do occur, usually at the worst possible moment, and the big bonus is that some manufacturers offer free service for the first couple years of ownership. What this really means is that you will absolutely know how much your car expense is going to be every month, no surprises.

Fact: you can lease a new car for the same monthly payment as it would cost you to buy a used car. Maybe less.

I mentioned liability above and what I mean about that is this: What do you think happens to the value of your car after its been in an accident? That's right, It goes down.

Say you bought your car 5 years ago and you just paid it off. You own it free and clear and want to keep it another year to stockpile some cash for that new Camaro that just came out. Everything is fine till the day you're broadsided by the guy texting his girlfriend and your insurance company elects to repair your car instead of totaling it. Your down payment on that new Camaro just went way down because the value of your current car just went down by almost half.

If you're dead set on buying and owning your car here's how to do it.

Whether you lease or buy, get a car with good resale value or residual value. Here's a website that tells you which cars have good resale. You'll notice that there are almost no American made cars on the list. There's a reason some cars have a higher resale than other cars and as I said before it's one of the best indicator of the quality of an automobile.

http://blog.truecar.com/2012/12/06/truecar-and-alg-reveal-new-car-residual-values/

The goal of owning your car is the thought of no car payments right? And it is possible, you buy a car, get a great interest rate and pay it off in 5 years and for the next five years you have no payments and relatively no problems. Now you have a ten year old car and it's time to get another one. Your car is now worth a couple thousand bucks, maybe a little more, so you've got a little toward a down payment on a new one. Take the money you get from trading in your car, combine it with a little cash and upgrade to the next model. Now you've got a nicer car for basically the same payment you had on the one you just traded. Also, if you've been smart and have been putting some money away for the rainy day when the transmission went out and it never did then you have a little nest egg that you can throw at the new car as well. Or take just a little of the money you've been saving and lease a new car, then take the rest and do something smart like make an investment in something worthwhile. Start an IRA or a take a trip to Jamaica.

If you treat your car like it's an expense and not an investment you'll have a clear understanding of the relationship. I treat my car as my monthly transportation expense and I allocate a certain dollar amount to it every month.

Next, we'll talk about some of the pitfalls that can happen at the dealership in regards to leasing and purchasing and some of the tricks dealers play to get you to buy a car today.

Tricks of the Trade

When you lease a car you always make the first payment that day along with the DMV fee. These are called the "drive offs" and when you walk out you've only got 35 payments left (assuming you did a 36 month lease). Whether you give them any money or not the first payment is always made the day the contract is signed. You can absolutely do a "no money out pocket lease," notice I didn't say "no money down" because money down, or down payment is treated a little differently when you lease. They call it "cap reduction" and without getting into a lot of detail cap reduction is anything you give over and above the "drive offs." All you need to ask when discussing a lease with a dealer and he's giving you a quote is how much "out of pocket"?

Here's a simplistic example:

Structure of a 36 month lease with drive offs out of pocket

Sale price: $19,999.00 (cap cost)

Drive offs: $325.91 + $169.00 = $494.91 [first payment of $299 + tax ($26.91) + DMV fee ($169)]

Monthly payment: $299 + tax = $325 .91

You would write a check for $494.91 and then have 35 payments remaining of $325.91

Same scenario with $0.00 money out of pocket

Sale Price: $ 19,999.00

Drive offs: $494.91

Cap cost: $20,493.91 (the cap cost goes up because you're not making the drive off payment and it gets rolled into the sale price, the dealer is making it for you)

Monthly payments: with $0.00 money out of pocket your payment will be $349.89 including tax for 35 months.

When quoting lease terms I use "out of pocket" and when quoting a payment I say "including tax" because that's really all you care about. How much money do I need to give you now to take this car home and how much is it going to cost me every month?

A common trick dealers play is the "down payment" and "plus tax" game. It goes like this:

You're negotiating a lease and the dealer gives you a quote that says

$2,000.00 down and $350 a month. You agree. He sends your stuff into the business manager (the F & I guy) and they shuttle you into the F & I office to sign. He collects your two thousand dollars and then asks you how you'd like to handle the first payment and the DMV fee. You look at him dumbfounded and ask "what are you talking about?" He explains that on a lease you always have to make the first payment the day you consummate the deal. You begrudgingly hand over another 700.00 bucks. Then he produces the contract for you to sign (after he tries to sell you another product called GAP insurance) and you notice that the $350 payment has now gone up to $381.50. Upon questioning our friendly finance manager he replies "Oh, it was $350...... plus tax. You always have to pay tax," he says as he looks at you like you were born yesterday. "Of course, what was I thinking" you say and proceed to sign the contract and wander out to drive away in your new car. What In fact happened was they increased their profit by another $1,700 by bumping you the $700 on drive offs and the $30 a month on payment. The salesman's commission just went up another $400.00 and he'll be high fiving the manager after you leave.

When you discuss lease terms with a car dealer always make them commit to terms of "how much out of pocket" and "how much including tax." I've seen it happen too many times. I've lost business because another sales guy beat my quote by not including drive offs and sales tax.

The Switch

There's an old story about a legendary salesman on his death bed, his protégé is sitting beside the bed holding his hand in the last hours. He asks the old legend, "Harvey, how'd you do it? How'd you sell so many cars in your lifetime? I mean you were the greatest." The old legend motions for the young man to lean in close so he can impart his words of wisdom and whispers "Switch em," and then dies.

The "switch" can be applied to anything. Usually a customer will come in with a general idea about what they're looking for and what they want to pay. And it's likely they've done some research on it. If you can switch them off that research you've taken the driver's seat. They now have no idea what a good deal might look like on that particular item. I used to offer a switch the moment I met somebody. They say, "I want to look at a Ford Explorer" As we were walking to look at Explorers I would casually walk them past an Expedition and say "Aren't those nice?" "Yeah, they are." And keep walking. Then I might ask them "Were you thinking about leasing or buying?" When they came in they were thinking about buying; now they might be thinking about leasing merely because I mentioned it. Later on, in the showroom I'll throw in the switch. "Here's how much the Explorer is, but here's how much you can lease that $45k Expedition for, and it won't be that much different, and…. the Expedition may and probably will lease for less than a purchase on an Explorer." Got em, and I just made a pounder!

35

Switch 'em on cars. Switch 'em from a buy to a lease. Switch 'em from a lease to a buy... any switch will increase profit and put more commission in my pocket.

Don't fall for the switch until you're given all the information that goes along with it and even then you should go home and think about it.

The switch will take place at any time during your visit. I used to plant the seed for the switch the moment we met and then throw it in at the appropriate moment when you were ripe for it. But the switch can take place in the finance office too after you already done the negotiating and your defenses are down. You go into see the finance guy to type your paperwork and he'll switch you while you're there in front of him and the computer.

I once had a finance manager switch my customer from a new car to a used car while they were in his office doing paperwork on the new car we had negotiated. I couldn't believe it and neither could the other managers. I tried to get him fired for it as this was truly under handed. He hadn't even looked at the car and neither had the client but here they were buying it anyway. Of course the management looked the other way as he had increased the stores profit significantly (and my commission too) but this wasn't the point. We then saw this customer every other week because there were problems with this particular used car, and of course they never bought another car from us again, but hey, they made a pounder. I, on the other hand, lost the good will and trust of the person who referred the customer to me and it took months to reassure him that this would never happen again. The dealership probably lost five sales in order to increase the profit on one deal. Make sense? Not to me it doesn't, but remember, that's how these guys operate.

A quick note about leasing and money factors.

When you lease a car they use what's called a "Money Factor" and it's just a fancy term for interest rate, but... on a lease contract the dealer is not required to disclose the money factor. When you buy (purchase, not lease) a car the terms are clearly spelled out on the contract. Price, down payment, interest rate and term (how long the contract is) are all clearly mentioned on the contract. On a lease contract they will not tell you what interest rate you're paying. Money Factors are not disclosed, and are calculated using funny numbers like .00240, what does that number mean to you?... right... nothing. You have no idea what rate of interest you're actually paying. You can do a quick calculation to turn that money factor into an interest rate by multiplying by 2400 as follows: .00240 X 2400= 5.76. On a lease payment with a .00240 money factor the interest rate you're paying is 5.76%.

Note: When there is a factory sponsored incentive on a lease they'll use really low money factors, I've seen them as low as .00001, that's .024% interest, or basically 0 %, we like these kinds of money factors. Manufacturers will also use alternate term lengths to make payments more attractive, for example they'll use a 27 month term or a 39 month term. Keep in mind that you will have to renew your registration in order to keep the car those additional months. It may not be worth it to pay for a whole year's registration just to drive a car an additional three months.

Test Driving

Case study: Hillary, mid 30's mom of 2 rambunctious boys. Owns her own business

I love Hillary, she's pretty and smart. I've known her a long time and she only buys her cars from me now. But before she met me she and her husband went to test drive a new Honda Odyssey because their second child was on the way.

What happened? They only went in to test drive; they were going to drive a Honda and a Toyota before they made a decision.

4.5 hours later with a tired, hungry, screaming kid they drove out in the new Honda in a 60 month lease. They were buried in that van and had to give it back at the end of 5 yrs because they didn't own it.

Why did they do it? Because the sales person wasted so much of their time that they didn't ever want to go through this again, were so tired and worn out they did it to get it over with.

First of all let me say that I have never test driven a new car. It's new, there's nothing wrong with it, it'll drive fine and unless you have some medical condition there's no need to drive it. If you're looking at mid-sized sedans in a particular price range they will all have similar features and for the most part they will all be comfortable. The only time I drive a car is if it's the one I'm going to take home.

Everything a salesman does from the moment you walk on the lot is choreographed to get you to pick a car out of stock and take it home today, from the walk around, to the test drive to the sitting down and sharing numbers.

The walk around is where the salesman literally walks you around the car and describes it features and benefits. The walk around starts at the left front quarter panel of the vehicle then moves under the hood where the salesman will tell you about crumple zones and other safety features designed to protect you in case of an accident, it winds around the whole car where it ends at the driver's seat where you will be asked to take a seat so we can give it a test drive. Dealers and Manufacturers literally have walk around competitions with cash prizes.

The walk around and test drive are a ploy to get you to fall in love with the car. Let's face it, new cars are nice, they smell nice and they drive nice, and if you've been driving a beater for the last couple years you're going to be influenced. If the salesman is smart he won't say too much during the test drive. I used to only say a couple things on the test drive aside from giving directions, one of them was "Can you imagine pulling up to your house in this new car?" They of course would imagine pulling up to their house in this new car, they've started to take mental ownership already, it works.

After the test drive you'll be led into the showroom and asked to sit down. He'll pull out a piece of paper called a four square and a credit app. The salesman's only job at this point is to get you to make a commitment, any commitment, even a ridiculous commitment. (a $150.00 dollars a month for that $40k SUV?) Once you've made a commitment chances are good that you'll be leaving in a car. In the car business we call it "would you took em" or "if I could, would you?" The salesman will say " well, If I can get my manager to take this ridiculous offer your making you'll take this car home today right?" Once you've said yes to this question you have officially (mentally) decided to buy a car, they'll get to a number that is acceptable to them if by nothing more than wearing you out. Don't buy into the "commitment" game.

How do you avoid the commitment game? Don't go to the dealership is how.

You've decided what type of car you want and narrowed down the field. You know you want a new hybrid, are considering the Honda and Toyota. You want to drive both to get a feel for them.

Here's what I would do.

Sales people hate test drives, especially if they think you're not buying today. I've literally seen salesmen tell customers to "hang on while I get the keys" and then never come back, leaving you standing there in the heat while he has a smoke in the back lot with his buddies.

The best advice I can give here is to go rent the cars you're thinking about buying. Rent it for a day and drive it around. May cost you 30 bucks but it'll be well worth it. Rental companies have just about every make and model available, even high end stuff like Lexus and Mercedes. It may take a couple phone calls but it'll be worth it in the long run as you don't have to go deal with a sales guy and you can drive it for more than 5 minutes. Some dealers even have rentals available, check and see if the local dealer rents cars for their service customers.

What if you live in an area where they don't rent the kind of cars you want to buy and absolutely have to go to the dealer? Make an appointment.

Remember I said to try and avoid going to the dealership and that if you do to make sure you know why you're there and what you want to accomplish in the shortest amount of time possible.

Call ahead and ask to speak with the fleet or internet manager. Tell them you'd like to test drive a particular car and ask if they have one in stock. Yes? Great, I'll be down on my lunch break to take it for a drive; can you have it ready for me? Super, can I ask for you? Great be there in 20 minutes.

What this does is help you avoid the gauntlet. Now you have the name of someone to ask for when you're approached by one of the liners guarding the kingdom. You have also given them a time limit for your visit, your lunch break. They know you only have an hour for lunch so you're not going to be buying any cars on this visit. This will also give you an idea of how professional this particular dealership is. If the guy is waiting for you when you arrive, if the vehicle is ready to go when you get there, these are good signs. If you arrive and the guy is not around or he has to go hunt for keys, if when you go to get in the car the battery is dead and he has to find the jumper box and jump the car to get it started, these are not good signs, or if the guy makes you wait while he goes and gets a car. If you stand around for more than 10 minutes it's time to leave. You had prefaced your conversation on the phone with "I'm on my lunch break." You don't have time to be standing around waiting for him to get his act together. Now the fleet or Internet manager may hand you off to a salesman for the test drive but it should still be handled professionally and quickly, don't be offended by this as they are managers and may not do test drives, but they are the guys who can give you numbers on the sale price of the car. Get their contact info.

Do not discuss numbers while you're there. I'll say it again; do not discuss figures while you're there to test drive. Take the salesperson's business card and make sure you have their email address. Thank them politely for their time and let them know you'll be in touch once you've made a decision on what kind of car you'll be buying. I would also suggest you don't discuss the other cars that you're thinking about test driving.

Trade-Ins and Used Cars

Case Study:

Katie, - self employed, financially stable with a good income and a great job. And...my lady.

Katie went to look at the new VW beetles when they came out and fell in love. She leased a Turbo Beetle Convertible (Harvest Moon I think the color was..... very pretty!) and traded in her aging Toyota 4runner, It had about 70,000 miles on it and was in good shape, she didn't need to get rid of it.

This is back when we were first dating and she didn't tell me she was going to go look at VW's. The next time we saw each other I noticed the new car and of course asked her a bunch of questions, such as where'd you get that? You know what I do for a living right?

She had traded in the 4Runner and put $1,000.00 along with it (about $5000 total) and left with what she thought were low payments ($390 a month) for 3 years. Do you see the problem here?

This was a big one. That Salesman is probably still in Hawaii on the commission he made off her.

So what happened: Katie was a "laydown" on the new car, He stole her trade and switched her to a lease. So many things wrong here I don't know where to start. This guy hit the jackpot all in one sale.

Let's start with the 4 Runner. Her trade: He gave her $4,000.00 dollars for a car that was worth at least 5, so he stole a thousand right there, then got another thousand out of her on top of that. I'm sure they marked the car up that 4000 over the sticker price when they leased it to her.

Every now and then a car comes along that will sell for more than the sticker price, the Corvette when it was re-designed. The Mazda Miata when it first came out sold for over the sticker price. Ferrari's will sell for $100,000.00 over the sticker price. The VW beetle was one of these as well but what generally happens is that over a short amount of time the price comes down as the availability increases. You can buy Beetles now for $100.00 over dealer cost (invoice).

How did he steal her trade? When you take a car to a dealer to trade in the salesman will take it to the Used Car Manager and he'll put a number on it, let's say $5000.00, The Used Car Manager acts as an independent third party and that's what he's willing to buy your car for. Anything under that number is profit for the dealer, so the sales manager (the King) will tell the salesman to tell the customer that his car is worth $4,000.00, if the customer says OK then the dealer just made an additional thousand on the car deal. This is one of the best ways to make additional profit on a car sale. New car profit margins are shrinking every year. You won't get the big discounts on new cars that you used to see, three and four thousand dollar discounts don't exist anymore. Some cars have less than a thousand dollars profit in them these days, so a dealer has to do what he has to do to make money and part of that is screwing you out of your trade-in.

The Used Car Managers job is to keep the used car lot full, and there are several ways to do it. He'll buy cars from Enterprise rent-car or other rental car companies. He has some shady friends who are wholesalers, who bring cars by for him to look at and possibly buy, and he'll go to the auction as well, but his best and cheapest source is trade-ins. He can take trade-ins cheaply because he knows the people want to get out of them and don't want to deal with having to sell them on their own so he'll lowball your trade and try to steal it, so he sends an already lower bid to the sales manager when he appraises a trade. The sales manager will then "under allow" on the trade to the salesman working the deal with the customer, he'll give the customer a lower number than what the used car manager gave him. The Used Car Manager has committed his $5,000 to the trade, that's what he's buying it for. It's like two separate businesses in one. A really aggressive sales manager will "shop the trade" after the deal's done and the customer has left. He'll call other dealers and see who's willing to give him the most for his car, thereby making more profit on the trade (called Gross). This may piss off used car managers but will help keep them honest. Of course the customer will see none of this additional money.

The best way to find out what your car (trade-In) is really worth is to look on the Internet AND get it appraised. I've found that CarMax is a great resource for used car values and told most of my customers to go there first before coming to see me with the car they want to trade in. They provide a printout of what they're willing to buy your car for and it's good for a week. CarMax is nationwide and a growing company with new locations opening all the time. They've become strong competition for car dealers that sell used cars, and they all do. Car dealers use various sources to determine used car values; Kelly Blue Book is used in the West, the Black Book in other parts of the Country.

If Katie had gone to CarMax before she went to the VW store she would have known her Toyota 4Runner was worth anywhere from 5-7,000 wholesale. Dealers buy cars wholesale by the way, not retail. Retail her car was worth over $10K, meaning if she had sold it on her own she probably could have gotten close to that, instead of the $4k the dealer gave her. But selling a car privately is a pain the rump sometimes. Trading it in is a lot easier and dealers know this.

Next, he switched her from a buy to a lease. Now remember leasing is not a bad thing but in her case it was. She had bought and paid off her Toyota and now traded it in on a lease. That was on a car she was going to have to give back to the bank. She got nothing for it and I might add, 4Runners have great resale value and are easy to sell privately because people want them.

What should she have done?, Well, if she *had* to trade the 4Runner in then I would have made them give me money back for it, take only a portion of the trade in value and apply it to the new car and have them cut me a check back for the difference. And I would not have given them any additional money. I would have negotiated the price of the Beetle over the phone before I even went in to look at it, and really, I would have kept the trade-in and sold it privately or just kept it. A great second car to have.

Now the fact that she leased the Beetle was a good thing, 2 ½ years into the lease the tail lights had gone out several times. They're only covered for the first year by the way. Further, on her way to the dealer the car simply quit running while she was driving, a scary proposition for anybody, but luckily she was on a residential street and it was no big deal. She coasted to the curb and called the dealer to come get it.

So what do you think happened when the lease was up on that Beetle? Yep, she leased another VW, a Turbo Diesel this time. I said "You didn't learn your lesson the first time?" Nope, and she loved that diesel until she had the same kind of problems with it. That's one of the good things about leasing too; you're never stuck with these things forever.

Upside down?

When you owe more on your car than it's worth we call that being "upside down." In real estate I've heard it called "being under water" and it only happens when there's a payoff on the car. If you own your car free and clear you can't be upside down. That being said some people get into a position of wanting to get new car before their current one is paid off. Unless there's a really good reason to I wouldn't do it for it gets you into a hole that's very hard to dig out of. I've seen it happen more times than it should and usually by the time you get to me it's too late and the only thing I can do is tell you that you have to ride it out until all your payments have been made and then start over with a different car and never do that again.

What ends up happening is the dealer will roll any inequity or remaining payments into the new car deal. Remember this is basic economics, there is no free lunch and dealers are not going to eat your remaining payments or inequity no matter what they tell you. You hear the ads on the radio, we'll pay off your car no matter how much you owe!" Of course they will, you're paying for it. "Oh, they're going to make my last payments for me." No, they're not. You're still going to make them. They will simply roll those payments into the new purchase or lease. Remember there are no deals! And I'm always amazed at how often I hear this. "They said they'll make the last payments for me, how are they going to do that?" The money or payments are still owed and unless you get a letter from the bank saying they'll waive your remaining payments they will get paid.

How do you know if you're upside down?

Call the bank that's financing the car and ask them what the payoff is. They'll give you a number that's good for specific amount of time, usually ten days. This number is what you owe on your car if you wanted to pay it off today. Now go to KBB.com and find out the trade-in value of your car. Remember that you may not get exactly what KBB says your car is worth but this will give you an idea. If the numbers are close then you can investigate getting into a new car, if you owe a lot more on your car than what it's worth better to wait till you get closer to paying it off.

Used Cars:

I mentioned used cars earlier and said that they can be a good buy. The problem with used cars is that there is not set cost on a used car, meaning we have no idea what the dealer paid for it. When I negotiate a car deal I like to negotiate the dealer's profit, knowing what they paid for it is the only way to do this. I don't trust car salesmen as far as I can throw them, and I know that used cars are a big profit center for car dealers. Where a dealer will take a 100 dollar profit on a new car they generally won't take less than a thousand on a used car and they like to average about 2500 per used car. Remember where I said dealers get used cars from. They get them from wholesalers, rental car companies, the auctions and trade-ins. Your best deal on a used car is going to be one they took in on trade. That will be the one they most likely paid the least for, remember they like to steal trades.

You're going to have to do a lot more research on a used car than on a new one. New car Invoice information is readily available on the Internet as well as the incentive information. You can negotiate with confidence on a new car because we know what the dealer paid for it.

Not so with used cars. Two dealers can have the same used car and the price can be thousands of dollars in difference because we have no idea what they paid for it or how long it's been on the lot. Dealers tend to be willing to take less profit on a used car that's been there for 30 days or more. These are all questions I would ask when talking to a sales guy about a used car. How long has it been here? Was it a trade –in?

But before you buy it do research. Look on the Internet and see what other dealers are asking for similar cars. Go to KBB.com and see what the car is worth as a trade-in to a dealer. This might give you an idea of what he may have taken it in for, but he probably had to do some reconditioning to it, new tires, etc. Also ask the dealer what was done to the car to make it ready for sale; did they put new tires on it? Or paint a quarter panel?

Should you buy from a private party? Buy a car from a private party or someone off the street and you'll definitely get a better price than a car on a dealer's lot but you're buying the car as is. There's a pretty good chance that car is going to need something. Take it to a mechanic, someone you trust or if you don't have someone you trust take it to the dealer and ask how much they'll charge you to do an evaluation on the car. Shouldn't be more than 100 bucks and it will be well worth it. They'll be able to tell you if the car has been in an accident and if there's anything it might need in the near future.

A note about salvaged title cars.

Don't ever buy one! Plain and simple. Don't ever buy a car with a salvaged title. What that means is that the car was totaled by an insurance company and somebody rebuilt it to resell and make money on. Whenever I took a car in on trade and found out it had a salvaged title the appraised value went down by half. If the car was worth ten thousand it was now worth five or less! Salvaged title cars will have a note on the actual pink slip or physical title that says 'SALVAGED". Stay away!

The Big Secret: Buy A Car In An Hour Or Less

I was out of the car business for about 10 years from my early 20's till my early 30's while I ran my own business, I had figured out an early age that these guys did not have my best interest at heart. I had had shoulder surgery and needed to do physical therapy to rehab my arm. I remember distinctly how much grief they gave me about having to take time off for rehab. They didn't care if my arm was attached or not. Get out there and take an "up" was the response I got, and my dad was the owner of the place, the guy that signed their paychecks. It really does take a particular type of individual to sell cars.

I sold my business in the early 90's and needed a job, I know how to sell cars, I said to myself and got a job at my dad's old store. Within a month of working on the front line they asked if I'd be interested in running a newly formed dept. "The Internet Dept." They weren't convinced it would work but said if I sold ten cars I would get a bonus. They gave me a little desktop computer and set me up in a small office off the showroom. I didn't see or hear from management at all. That first month I sold thirty seven cars (a huge number) and the general sales manager was in my office every day from then on asking how many I was going to do that day. By the end of the first year I had added a partner and we were selling ninety cars a month.

Everybody asked what our secret was—how were we doing this? The average sales guy sells ten a month and the top guy in the store will generally sell twenty-five, maybe thirty. The big secret was that we were just being upfront and straightforward with our customers. We were giving prices over the phone and people were coming in and buying cars by the truckload.

This was back when the Internet was brand new and as I said the management was not convinced it would work at all. Well, it did. Now, every dealership has an Internet dept and they rely on it. The Internet dept in a dealership could be responsible for selling as much as a third of the dealership's total volume every month, but it still hasn't really changed the way they do business. When I was running the Internet dept back in the beginning I was generating as much profit per car deal as the retail dept, even more. We were making as much on each sale as they normally do because we were engaging the same old tricks and they worked even better because we were operating under the guise of being upfront with our pricing. I had gained the trust of the customer and was using it to my advantage.

Now you can use this to your advantage. Remember when I said to call ahead and make an appointment if you were going to take a test drive? I told you to get the contact info for that guy because you can use it later. Well now, is later.

You've decided what kind of car you want, you've run your credit and know that you have a credit score of 700+ and decided you want to lease a new Honda Accord or maybe a Toyota Prius. Call that guy up and get a quote. You've looked on KBB.com and you know how the vehicles are configured. Japanese cars are only configured certain ways, you probably can't get it exactly the way you want it. Write those numbers down and then call another dealer. Ask to speak with the fleet or Internet manager and ask him the same thing.

I usually ask for the fleet manager or "who handles your fleet sales?", but some stores may not have a fleet department. Fleet departments were set up so companies that buy multiple cars at a time or several cars over the course of a year could speak with someone directly without having to go through the retail process. They would have a contact at the dealership that could give them the information they need over the telephone. The transactions are handled differently than if you just walk in off the street, which is where the majority of dealership business used to come from, but not anymore.

 Internet Departments are set up in kind of the same fashion and have taken over the fleet duties in a lot of stores these days. The Fleet or Internet Manager will give you a price right over the phone or better yet, he'll email it to you. But make sure he's quoting you on a vehicle he has available. Anybody can quote a low price on a car that they don't have or have no intention of getting.

If you're paying cash or using outside financing get an out-the-door price. If you're financing get payments, know how much you want to put down and ask what interest rate he's using based on your 700+ credit score. If you're leasing, get payments including tax and how much out-of-pocket.

What you may find is that the quotes are not that far apart, fleet and internet pricing is very competitive nowadays and dealers operate on very slim margins. At the last dealership I worked in they were talking about changing their pricing policy. They wanted to quit giving prices over the phone and ask that the customers come in to get a price. I understand why, customers were just shopping prices and going to the guy with the lowest price. *Just because the guy has a lower price doesn't mean it's a better deal....*

It's really not about price.

If you've done your homework a hundred dollars will not be the difference between buying a car and not.

Case Study: *Anonymous Business Manager for Hot shot actor.*

I used to get a lot calls from business managers looking to buy cars on their clients behalf. Big time movie stars and celebrities typically don't do this car buying stuff themselves; they have their business managers do it.

So one day I get a call from a business manager, he's looking for a car for his new client. Keep in mind that this person had been referred to me by two different sources that I work with on an ongoing basis.

So this guy calls, tells me who he's working for and wants numbers on a new car, I give them to him right there while we're on the phone. I knew how much I was making on the car and it wasn't very much. This guy says "not good enough", I ask him where I need to be in order to make it happen, he won't tell me, just that he has a better number. So I come down another 7 bucks a month (I was literally selling the car at my cost now) and he says "still not good enough". I ask him again, where do I need to be? He still won't say. Needless to say I was getting a little pissed now and ended up hanging up on the guy, not my brightest moment. But this guy was such a jerk that I didn't care if he bought his car somewhere else. The point being that I was willing to sacrifice my hundred dollar commission (that's all we make on these give away deals) not to deal with this guy. Now he may have gotten a better deal but by how much? I was making nothing on the car, how much was the other guy losing in order to earn this guys business merely to say he had sold a car to a celebrity? Was that guy really going to provide the service that goes along with a sale after the car has been delivered?

The lesson here?

I said it before, there is more to buying a car than getting the best price. When someone says to me "what's your best price on a _____insert car name here____ ….." my wise guy answer is, "it's the one you take it home for…… Friend"

When negotiating a car deal you want to negotiate the dealer's profit, ask him what his cost is and ask to see the invoice if you're not convinced he's telling you the truth. Dealer invoice information is readily available on the Internet and accurate to within a few dollars, there's really no reason for him to lie to you, he knows this.

 A fair profit for a dealer can be anywhere from one hundred dollars over invoice to one thousand dollars over invoice depending on the car, the current availability and demand, and some cars may even be selling for sticker price and over. The market will drive the price and I've seen cars selling for as much as one thousand below dealer cost. When a manufacturer is vying for a specific goal like #1 selling car in America, the cars will be plentiful and heavily discounted. When Honda and Toyota were competing for #1 sales status you could buy a Camry or an Accord for well below the actual dealer cost. Don't look a gift horse in the mouth, take the money and run. But don't negotiate yourself out of a deal either.

I used to tell customers that my price is in direct correlation to how much I like you and it was true. If you squeezed me for every penny of profit I may not be so inclined to help you when you needed it, maybe when something went wrong. The service dept. is out that door sir.

Do you know how much $500 dollars equates to in a monthly car payment? If you're buying the car it adds up to about $12.00 a month, if you're leasing a car it comes to about $15.00 dollars a month.

Are you $100.00 away from making a car deal? That hundred bucks is about $3.00 a month in a car payment but may be the difference between a dealers saying yes or no to a deal. Do you really want to squeeze me that hard? It's supposed to be a win win situation

I figured that if I made an honest attempt to save you as much money as I could and helped you make an educated choice on financing and the proper car for your needs that you would come find me the next time you needed a car or you'd tell your friends that I was an honest guy and would take good care of them. For the most part that's what happened, I made a lot of new friends and they used me as their auto consultant. They will call me when it's time for a service appointment or when something happened to the car and if they were a loyal customer I would work with the service dept to take care of whatever problems they had. There were numerous occasions where the car was out of warranty and something went wrong that would cost more than a thousand dollars to fix and we got the manufacturer to cover it for free. There are benefits to knowing someone. Try calling the fly-by-night sales guy you bought your last car from for that kind of favor; I'll bet he doesn't even work there anymore.

So how do you find an honest guy?

Listen to your gut.

If a sales person answers your questions with a question it may be time to move on. Of course we need information to provide you an accurate quote but you'll know if someone is not giving you a straight answer.

The Negotiation -Wrap it up!

Case Study: the perfect experience!

Chuck calls, the lease is up on his current car, it's time for another one. OK, what color will it be this time?, we work out the details on the phone, confirm everything verbally. I go get the paperwork typed up, get the car washed and gassed and take it to his house, sign all the paperwork and take the lease return back to the dealer. He never had to leave his home or office and the whole thing took him probably an hour. I did it hundreds of times!

How do you negotiate the deal? The car business is like any other business in that its simple economics, the dealer has a product that he paid a certain amount for and he needs to sell it for more than he paid for it in order to stay in business. That's how you need to approach it when you talk to car dealers. If I wanted to buy a car different from the brand I was selling I would call the fleet manager at the store and ask him "Where are you guys on these Toyota Corollas right now?"Or "How much over Invoice can I get a new Toyota Corolla for?" If he doesn't answer my question pretty quickly and starts giving me a song and dance I'll thank him for his time and call another dealer. Same routine, I may not even tell him I work in the car business until later.

The conversation will go something along these lines. "The new 2013 Corolla LE has a sticker price of $16,479.00 my cost on it is $14,849.00, I'll let you have it for $200.00 over invoice, there's also a lease special at the moment so with no money out of pocket, the payments will be $249.00 a month plus tax or $269.00 including tax @ 12k miles a year, that work?"

So you've found a good guy who's been up front with you. He's emailed you the specs on the car he has in stock, on the ground now, and you've agreed on a price. It wasn't the lowest price you were quoted but you didn't really trust the other guy who gave you a lower number but not the exact car you wanted.

What do you do now?

Offer to let him send you a credit application and tell him you'll fill it out and email it back to him. After he runs your credit and confirms everything you'd like to come down and pick up the car, can he have it ready and waiting? If he's a good guy he'll agree. You can scan and email your driver's license and insurance info as well.

When you get to the dealer the car should be gassed and washed and ready to go, if you're lucky he's had the paperwork typed but most likely they will want to run you through the finance office so he can try to sell you some back end items.

Front End/Back End

Salesmen, Sales managers, Finance managers and pretty much everybody all the way up the chain get paid on a percentage of the profit made on the sale of cars.

Salesmen are paid commission, generally in the neighborhood of 20-25% of the profit made on the sale of the car itself, this is called front end gross.

The finance manager or business manager gets paid on the back end gross of the car deal. Front end gross is the money made on the actual sale of the car, back end gross is the money made selling you extra items like warranties, GAP insurance and Alarms. For example, the car cost the dealer 20,500 and he sells it to you for 21,500, that's 1000 dollars front end gross. If the finance manager sells you a warranty and makes 1000 dollars on it that's back end gross but the total gross of that particular car deal is now 2000 dollars. The store pays the salesman off the front end and pays the finance guy off the back end. If the finance guy doesn't sell you a warranty does she still get paid? Nope, not really. He'll have to make it up on the next guy. But don't fret. The finance guys get lots of chances; they get to talk to every person that buys a car while a sales guy may talk to twenty people before he gets one that actually buys a car.

The minimum a salesman will make selling a car is $100.00 . It's called a mini. Salesmen take lots of minis and they hate them, that's why they run you through the system, to try and make as much per car as they can. Remember the average guy on the line sells ten cars a month. But the fleet or Internet guy sells as many as thirty or more. He's happy to take a mini deal, they all add up at the end of the month.

The sales managers, general sales managers and general managers get paid on everything, front end and back end, that's why you see these guys wearing Rolex watches and driving fancy cars, but the poor liners don't make nearly as much, and by the way, they do all the hard work climbing in and out of cars, moving cars to get the one you want, jump starting cars that have dead batteries, etc.

So off you go into the finance office where the guy types up your contract and the DMV paperwork so they can register your car for you. He's going to try and sell you some stuff too.

Additional Items like warranties or GAP insurance are called back end items and they aren't necessarily a rip off.

Extended Warranties

If you're buying your car not leasing, you might want to think about an extended warranty. It'll generally extend the manufacturer's warranty by double what comes with the vehicle originally. Dealers love selling warranties, they make money on them and if they have a skinny deal on the car itself they can make up a little by selling a warranty and may even be willing to sell the car for less if you tell them you're your interested in a warranty as well. But don't let them fool you here either; the price of the warranty is just as negotiable as the price of the car. They'll try to sell it to you for $2500.00 bucks or more in some cases. Its generally worth about half that and the dealer will still make some money on it.

Do you need an extended warranty? It's a tough call, you may never use it but, if you use it once it will most likely pay for itself. New cars today are pretty much computer run. It's much easier to take it in and have the oil changed rather than do it yourself, and if something does go wrong with the car they'll need to plug the car into another computer and that will tell the mechanic what's wrong with the car. It will most likely be expensive.

You can negotiate this before you go into the dealership as well. Talk about the different warranties available, they'll come with different mileage and time configurations with the cheapest being the additional three years and 35,000 mile extension all the way up to eight years and 150,000 miles total time and mileage from when you buy the vehicle. Warranties are transferable also, meaning if you sell the car to someone else, the warranty will go with it. That's added value, my friends and worth a little something extra to a prospective buyer.

New cars generally have a three year/36,000 bumper-to-bumper warranty included when you buy them. If you want to double this warranty to six years/75,000 miles it shouldn't cost more than $1000.00. If you want to get the longer warranty don't pay more than $2000.00. They'll try to tell you that it cost $3,000.00 or more for the longest warranty but don't listen. An eight year 150,000 extended warranty is worth about $1,800-$2,000 and it is worth it!

GAP Insurance:

Gap insurance is another product idea somebody came up with in order to make more money. It works essentially like this: When you lease a car you generally don't put very much money down if any at all. If by some act of fate the vehicle is totaled in an accident before the lease is up your insurance company may not cover the whole amount owed on the vehicle to the bank. Meaning, your insurance company may not completely pay off the car and leave you responsible for the difference, hence the gap.

An example: You lease a new BMW 3 series, the minute you drive it off the lot it's worth 25% less than what you just paid for it, so you now owe $40k for a car that's now worth around $31-32K, and you wreck it, the insurance company says it's a total loss but that the cars only worth $32,000.00, but you owe $40,000.00 to the bank on it? That $8,000.00 is the "GAP" and you're responsible for it. Do you want to come up with $8,000.00 dollars just to get out of a car you just leased? No way Jose, but here's a solution. You can purchase GAP insurance to cover that difference, Mr. Customer. And its only $800.00 bucks making your payment go up only another $25.00 bucks a month. How's that for peace of mind?

My experience has been that only one customer I ever sold a car too had an opportunity to use GAP insurance and I've sold thousands of cars. That one customer had the GAP insurance and then wrecked their car with only one year left on the lease. The Gap insurance company denied the claim saying that because the customer had been late on some of the monthly car payments they would not pay. There was a huge argument between the GAP insurance company, the customer and the dealership. The Gap insurance company finally paid the difference only when we, the dealer threatened to stop using their product. It did clearly state in the fine print on the GAP insurance paperwork that if the customer was late on car payments they were not required to pay the claim. Sounds like a bunch of crap to me right? You think I ever sold them another car? Nope but it wasn't a huge loss anyway. They had been a struggle to get financed initially and had financial troubles all along. But it took hours of my time to deal with them because the management at the store didn't care about it at all; they pawned it off from the moment the complaint came in. I got involved and pushed to get someone to take care of it... customer service at its best.

Some insurance companies include GAP insurance with their coverage these days, I would check with your insurance company to see if it is included in your coverage and this will eliminate the whole GAP insurance conversation when you're at the dealer.

Finance reserve

Dealers make money on financing too, just like they make money on cars. They buy the money from the bank and then mark it up and sell it to you just as if it were an actual product. For example: the bank buys the money at the bank for 4.5% APR, they then mark it up to 5.5% and write your loan at the new rate. The money they make on the loan is called finance reserve and the finance guy gets paid on that as well.

Banks have now put a cap on how much money a dealer can make on reserve for any one transaction. Think dealers were taking advantage of the situation? You bet they were!

This finance signing papers process shouldn't take more than 15-25 minutes. If you have a trade-in it will take a little longer, but if you're in there for more than 30 minutes it's too long. When you're finished the finance guy will page your sales guy and you're basically done. He'll come get you and escort you out to your new car. Voila! There it is all shiny and new. He'll spend as much time as you need showing you how all the fancy new gadgets work and then send you home.

The whole thing should take less than an hour and if you have a trade-in maybe a little more. Hopefully everything went smoothly and you have confidence in your new friend. Put him in your contact list and refer him business. When it's time for your first service appt. call him and ask him who he likes out in the service dept, see if he'll make the appt. for you, it'll save you time out there as well.

Hopefully he'll still be working at the same store when it's time for you to get another car, or when your wife or your kid needs a new one.. This can turn into a long term relationship and you'll have a friend inside the system.

OR... you can call me and I'll do all the hard work for you.

Info@buyacarin1hour.com

Buying a car is not that difficult as long as you're prepared. The investment of time in doing research is not that difficult either with all the information available on the Internet. If you go into this with a clear understanding of what your goal is you'll do fine.

Choose a quality car that has good resale value. Know what your credit looks like before you talk to a dealer.

Call a few different guys and see how they treat you then reward the salesman for his honest behavior.

Conduct the transaction over the phone and via email and let them know what your expectations are in regards to your time and that you want to be out of there within an hour.

Hopefully you'll find someone you can trust for years to come and you'll both benefit from the relationship.

Glossary of Terms:

ACV: Actual cash value, this is the number they'll apply to your trade in. The ACV is how much the used car manager is willing to give you for your trade.

Buy Rate: the actual rate the dealer can get you financed at. What he pays for his money.

Cap Cost: includes the negotiated price of the vehicle plus any add-on fees or taxes that will be financed (not paid up front). It might also include the balance of a previous loan on a trade-in vehicle or the first payment and DMV fees (Drive offs). In a loan, it would be called "financed amount" but leasing has its own peculiar language.

Cap Reduction: Any money given to the dealer over and above the drive off fees (Leasing)

Dealer Invoice: what the dealer paid for the car

Domestic Content: percentage of parts on a vehicle that are manufactured in the US.

Drive Offs: Fees associated with leasing a car, generally include the first payment and registration fee and maybe a security deposit.

Finance Reserve: back end profit the dealer makes on your financing. It's just like a car in that he pays a certain amount for the financing he sells you and marks it up...i.e.... if he pays 4% for his money he'll sell it to you for 5% and take a point for himself.

Foreign Content: percentage of parts on a vehicle that are manufactured outside the United States.

Green Pea: A brand new sales guy with no experience

Gross: gross profit, the actual profit made from selling a car, Front end gross is what they made on the car itself; Back End Gross is what they made selling warranties and items offered to you in the finance office.

High-Ball: telling you your trade in is worth more than it really is so you'll have to come back after you've been to 10 other dealers.

Lay Down: a customer that comes in and doesn't negotiate, Dealers love laydowns!

Liner: guy that works on the front line at the dealership, the first guy you'll meet when you go to the   dealership.

Low-Ball: either quoting you a price so low on their new car that they know no one will beat it, or hitting your trade in below what it's really worth. Dealers will do this when they know you're not buying a car today, they'll low ball you so you have to call them back.

Money Factor: lease rate (interest rate) charged by the bank shown as a decimal number i.e.... .0024, converts to an interest rate by multiplying by 2400 or (.0024 X 2400 = 5.76% interest)

MSRP: Manufacturer's Suggested Retail Price, or... the Sticker price for a car posted clearly on the window of the new car.

Pounder: Salesman made a homerun sale, sold the car for sticker price or more and stole the trade-in

Residual: The amount you can buy the car for at the end of the lease, should be printed right on the contract when you lease the car.

Stealing the trade: gave the customer less for the trade-in than the used car manager appraised it for. Also called Under Allowing

Under Allow: giving the customer less for their trade in than what the used car manager appraised it for. *Note: sometimes dealers have to over allow on a trade too…meaning giving the customer more for their trade than it's worth because they owe the bank so much on it.*

UP: a customer that comes on the lot is an "UP" i.e…. that's my UP, or… Who's Up is that? What happened to that UP?

UPSIDE DOWN: When you owe more on your trade in to the bank than what it's really worth.

VIN: Vehicle Identification Number, 17 digits long and located in the door jamb, under the hood and at the base of the driver's side of the windshield viewable through the windshield from the outside

www.ingramcontent.com/pod-product-compliance
Lightning Source LLC
Chambersburg PA
CBHW070813290526
45795CB00002B/701